LOS ANGELES

A PICTURE BOOK TO REMEMBER HER BY

Designed by
DAVID GIBBON

Produced by
TED SMART

CRESCENT

INTRODUCTION

Sprawling northwards over the Santa Monica Mountains and south towards the Pacific, the vast metropolis of Los Angeles has grown phenomenally during the past decades to become one of America's most dynamic and exciting cities. Often referred to as 'The Big Orange', L.A.'s segments – places of entertainment, businesses, pleasure spots – are scattered throughout the metropolis and connected by one of the most intricate freeway systems ever seen.

The origins of the 'City of Angels' lie in the Pueblo, a small plaza retaining a delightful Spanish atmosphere, which has now become part of a 42-acre site preserved as a State Historical Landmark. It was from this site that El Pueblo de Nuestra Señora La Reina de los Angeles was proclaimed in 1769 by Father Juan Crespi, a member of the Spanish Expeditionary Force, headed by Gaspar de Portola, which was searching the area for possible mission sites. The early inhabitants of the tiny settlement soon discovered that the climate and soil of their new land was remarkably productive of grain and the vast, empty acres particularly suitable for cattle and horse breeding.

As tales of the richness of the soil began to spread, the influx of settlers was drawn by the opportunities afforded by the fertile region and the climate and, after the discovery of gold in the Sierra Nevada, in 1849, brought a rapid increase in the population of San Francisco. As 'gold fever' mounted, the demand for food, which the Los Angeleno ranchers were able to supply, turned the rural community into a busy and rowdy cattle town. A period of lawlessness and vice ensued as prospects of easy money drew an overflow of people from the north, but by the time the transcontinental railroad had arrived from Chicago, via Santa Fe, life had become more stable and the new arrivals, many of them farmers from the Midwest, developed the lush orchards started by the Spanish fathers.

Two new developments then changed the destiny of Los Angeles: the discovery of oil and the acquisition of San Pedro, a coastal town which was developed as an artificial harbour – paid for by the rich oil which gushed from an abundance of wells – and made the city not only an important industrial centre but also a thriving seaport.

The most important development of all, however, occurred just before World War I, when a group of enthusiasts armed with cameras converged in the California sunshine and started what was to explode into the multi-billion dollar film industry – and transformed the city into a glittering glamour centre – its focal point glossy Hollywood. Its stars were created by a vast publicity machine which made their lives as familiar as those of the public's own families, and their sumptuous homes in Beverly Hills became shrines to the 'greats' of the 'silver screen'.

Today Hollywood retains its prestigious position as a successful television film production centre, and millions of tourists still flock there; to walk along fabulous Sunset Strip and Hollywood Boulevard where bronze medallions commemorate the names of well-known actors of radio and television as well as of film; to visit Manns Chinese Theater and see the hand and footprints of some of its greatest stars cast in concrete; to see, at the Wax Museum, international personalities frozen in wax, and of course, to visit the exciting studios where tours of the lots, by special 'glamour trams', are conducted by aspiring actors and actresses. High in the hills is sited the Hollywood Bowl, a beautiful amphitheatre, and home of the Los Angeles Philharmonic, which performs its famous 'symphonies under the stars' during the summer season.

Los Angeles abounds with a wealth of attractions that draw more than nine million people every year; places such as Alligator Farm, Magic Mountain Pleasure Park and Knotts Berry Farm, where the spirit of adventure of the 'Old West' is revived in the Ghost Town and visitors can pan for gold, board a stagecoach or ride on the Rio Grand Calico Railway.

Of all the showplaces, however, one of California's most visited attractions is the extravaganza of Disneyland, 27 miles south of L.A., at Anaheim. Created by Walt Disney, this magical park is a wonderland guaranteed to keep adults spellbound and the young wide-eyed. Divided into six main themes, the park brings to life the film characters beloved by young and old alike, and at the end of each day provides a firework display every bit as fabulous as the kingdom of fantasy itself.

Within the heart of L.A. beautiful parks like MacArthurs, its lake cut by the renowned Wilshire Boulevard as it curves its way to the coast at Santa Monica, and the extensive Griffith Park, with its unique Zoo, provide plentiful leisure-time activities for the residents of the city.

For those anxious to escape from the turmoil of the city and its smog-filled skies, however, there are the magnificent coastal resorts to the west, lapped by the surf of the Pacific Ocean. Here Santa Monica, Malibu Beach and Long Beach, home of the retired ocean-liner the 'Queen Mary', now maintained as a museum, provide such a need.

Although sport is an important aspect of Los Angeles life, with its important educational establishments having outstanding facilities, cultural pursuits are equally as important and are evidenced in the superb Central Library; the Huntington Library, which has one of the largest collections of rare books and manuscripts and the impressive Museum of Art; whilst one of the most extraordinary private collections of art can be seen in the fabulous J. Paul Getty Collection, housed in his magnificent villa based on the plan of an ancient Roman villa.

The musical life of the city is centred at the superb Dorothy Chandler Pavilion, which, with the Mark Taper Forum and the Ahmanson Theater, provides a trio of buildings for theatrical entertainments.

This dynamic city, with its cosmopolitan atmosphere, perhaps owes some of its intensity for living to the ever-present threat of destruction, with the San Andreas fault, a major cause of earthquakes, just 30 miles away from the city centre. Yet in spite of the constant danger L.A.'s population is still increasing as the bright, magnetic orange continues to draw those with a dream who believe that it can be fulfilled in this great city of opportunity.

Flags *above and below* lend colour to the imposing heights of Century City.

The vast Harbour Freeway *left and overleaf* with its roaring traffic gives some idea of the enormity of America's third largest city, which at night *right* sparkles with a million lights.

o matter what the product or the
traction Los Angeles has an inbred flair
r the dramatic. In the Juschi fashion
ouse *on these pages* models display the
ost elegant fashions in the most
xurious surroundings whilst *overleaf*
rt of the Music Centre for the
rforming Arts, the Mark Taper Forum
mbines an imposing exterior with an
terior that permits an intimate theatre-
-the-round atmosphere.

The modern face of Los Angeles is reflected in its glossy buildings and expansive highways: *above* the City Centre and Harbour Freeway, *centre left* the intersection at Century Plaza and *below left* Hollywood and Vine. Traffic races past the Wilshire Building *above left,* while in more tranquil surroundings the graceful City Hall *right and below* stands serenely in the afternoon sunshine.

In Sunset Boulevard, the world famous 'Street of the Stars' *overleaf* neon signs advertise every conceivable attraction.

At night the illuminated splendour of Main Street and Broadway *above and centre left* or of Sunset Boulevard *above, right and below left* and the soft floodlighting of the Double Ascension *below* in Atlantic Richfield Plaza serve as reminders that this is still very much the 'Glamour City'.

The twin towers of Century City *overleaf* soar above the Century Plaza and Schubert Theatre.

t Beverly Drive and Olympic Blvd a onument *above* pays tribute to the film ars who strove for the preservation of everly Hills as a separate municipality. his independent municipality has been otly termed a 'residential city' because of s amazing collection of homes…each he eligible for inclusion in 'House eautiful', but Beverly Hills does have its ommercial establishments and restaurants hich like those elsewhere in Los Angeles flect all the luxury of the film star era at s zenith.

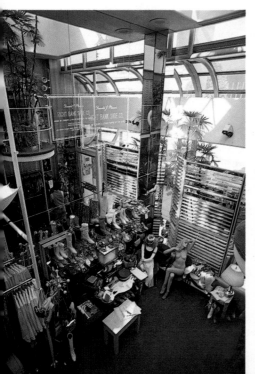

It is stores such as these that have earned Los Angeles its reputation as the manifestation of the American dream. This city seems to express the yearnings of people throughout the nation for glamour and the 'good life' and an essential part of that life as presented in glittering Rodeo Drive *on these pages* is occupied by cars like that displayed *above and right*…made entirely by hand and priced at $75,000.

In China Town *above, right and left* Los Angeles surrenders its modern look and assumes the Oriental flavour of an ancient culture with its pagoda-styled buildings set in an atmosphere heavy with the pungent aroma of Oriental food and incense.

In the forecourt of the Chinese Theatre, Hollywood *below right* the footprints, handprints and signatures of the movie stars of yesterday and today have been immortalized to form the city's most famous landmark.

The Hongwanji Buddhist Temple *overleaf* in Little Tokyo reflects all the ornate splendour of the East.

ith the passage of Hollywood's heyday
e nightlife of Los Angeles may seem
mparatively tame but despite the fact
at motion picture stars are no longer
mpelled to dress up each evening to be
en with other starlets or actor escorts,
e city still boasts an apparently endless
eam of night spots and clubs like the
ayboy Club *on these pages.*

neath a duo of steel and glass towers,
oadway Plaza in downtown *overleaf* is a
uristic two-level underground shopping
ll.

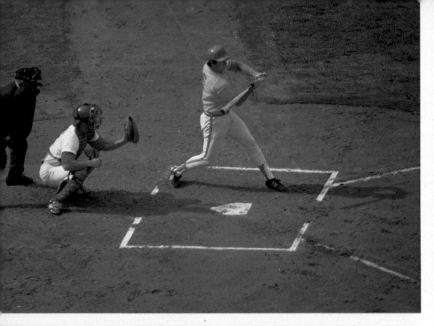

Watched from stands that seat 43,000 enthusiastic spectators, the Los Angeles Dodgers play the U. S. C. Trojans in a baseball match at Dodger Stadium.

the Bradbury Building *left* a huge
ylight floods the marble stairs and ornate
n railings with natural light. Built in
93 for a Mexican silver mining tycoon,
day it serves as a prestigious office
mplex.

s Angeles County Museum of Art *on
is page,* a complex of three modern
ildings at Wilshire Boulevard is
nsidered the finest art museum west of
e Mississippi.

walk along Rodeo Drive *overleaf left* or
it the Nance Mitchell Beauty Salon
erleaf right is to glimpse the distinctive
nd of fashion and luxury that has made
s Angeles the home of the stars.

The process of producing and publishing the Los Angeles Times, a paper which has the second largest circulation in the U.S.A. is an awesome operation, when viewed as here from behind the scenes.

The Bonaventure Hotel *above left* in
Figueroa Street is the creation of John
Pitman and the newest and most
spectacular addition to the downtown
scene, but the Victoria Station Restaurant
above, below left and right also offers a
plush and imaginative décor. Westwood
Village has a special relaxed atmosphere
and identity of its own which is reflected in
many of its innumerable restaurants *below*

The Movieland Wax Museum in Buena
Park was created by a film addict, Allen
Parkinson, who saw to it that some of the
most memorable film scenes were
recreated in exact detail in wax. *Overleaf:*
'The Awful Tooth'.

[t]he heart of Los Angeles lies the Pueblo *this page*, whose Mexican village [atm]osphere is most keenly felt in Olvera [Str]eet. Here in the sunshine, stalls can be [fou]nd laden with colourful merchandise [and] also cheerful street musicians who [fre]quently take part in the many festivities [hel]d in the area.

[T]he Botanical Gardens at Huntington [the] giant cacti grow to incredible [dim]ensions.

Mary's Gate Village *top left* at Long Beach is not far from the home of the 'Queen Mary', the famous ocean liner *on these pages* that completed her final voyage on December 9, 1967 after a 14,500 mile journey that took her around South America via Cape Horn.

Bought by the city of Long Beach at a cost of $3 million, the liner's attractions now include a three-level panorama created across the lower decks which reveals the world's largest marine exhibition, living sea exhibits designed by Jacques Cousteau, two malls of shops and three excellent restaurants.

Visitors can also tour the liner's Upper Decks with their luxury suites used during the Queen Mary's 31 years of Atlantic crossings.

Ports of Call Village, Whaler's Wharf in
San Pedro *above and below left* is a
unique tourist attraction reminiscent of
the old fishing communities and villages
of the early 19th century.

The Beverly Hills Hotel, Sunset
Boulevard *left* has a history intertwined
with that of the stars for it has been the
home from home for everybody from
kings and presidents of vast economic
empires to stars such as John Wayne and
Barbra Streisand.

Set in magnificent countryside *above
left* one of the canyon roads provides a
breathtaking view of Westwood Village
while the exotic Botanical Gardens of
Huntington *below* form part of a 200
acre estate in San Marino.

At Universal Studios in fabulous Hollywood *above right* visitors can take a two hour tram tour and delight in the make-believe world of the movies. Beverly Hills with its lovely old City Hall *below* and its Plaza *right* decorated with tropical palms and colorful blooms is the glamorous home for many of the stars of these movies.

Pasadena's ornate City Hall *below right* reflects the Spanish inspired architecture so prevalent in the 1920's and set among immaculate green lawns *above* imposing statues stand before the elegant Huntington Library.

The wonderful, magical world of Disneyland at Anaheim, captured *here and overleaf* with all the favourite Disney characters, from Mickey Mouse to Tigger, delights children and adults alike. Two of the most popular methods of transport in this fantastic wonderland are by monorail *above right* and by the delightful Mark Twain Riverboat *bottom right* which cruises down the river passing Tom Sawyer Island and Fort Wilderness.

Los Angeles' mild sunny climate encourages a wide variety of outdoor sports and every possible facility is made available for popular activities such as skateboarding.

Sunshine draws holiday-makers to the golden beaches of Santa Monica *left* and Malibu *below*, reputed to be two of the finest beach areas in Southern California and ideal for surfing and boating. Long Beach Marina *below right* provides idyllic moorings for pleasure craft and for those who prefer to remain on terra firma the pier at Santa Monica *above and right* offers a variety of entertainment.

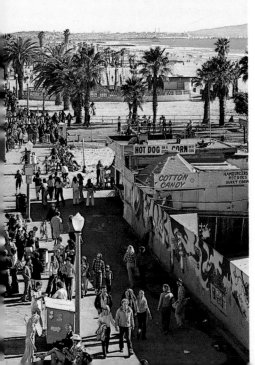

Nightfall brings a change of atmosphere and tempo as the sun sets on the beaches of Venice *above,* on Long Beach Marina *right* and on the exotic trees of beautiful MacArthur Park *below,* while the lights of Santa Monica pier *left* find their reflection in the waters of the Pacific Ocean.

The sunshine paradise of Malibu *overleaf,* noted for its famous movie colony, stretches along the West Pacific Coast Highway from the Los Angeles city line to the extreme frontier of Ventura County.

First published in 1979 by Colour LIbrary International Ltd.
© Illustrations: Colour Library International (U.S.A.) Ltd., 163 East 64th Street, New York 10021.
Colour separations by Fercrom, Barcelona, Spain.
Display and text filmsetting by Focus Photoset, London, England.
Printed by Cayfosa and bound by Eurobinder - Barcelona (Spain)
Published by Crescent Books, a division of Crown Publishers Inc.
Library of Congress Catalogue Card No. 79-87533
CRESCENT 1979